mrya
10/12

SPYING AND SECURITY

"..... but of course it *mustn't* go *any* further!"

CARELESS TALK COSTS LIVES

"CENSORED"

EXAMINED BY 42

Prvt. John Doe
U.S. Army.

FREE

Mrs. John Doe
1000 Silence St.
New Orleans, La.
U.S.A.

LET'S CENSOR
OUR CONVERSATION
About the WAR

WPA WAR SERVICES of LA

BROWN
BEAR
BOOKS

Published in 2011 by Brown Bear Books Limited
© Brown Bear Books Limited

Brown Bear Books Ltd.
4877 N. Circulo Bujia
Tucson, AZ 85718
USA
and
First Floor
9–17 St. Albans Place
London
N1 0NX

Brown Bear Books Ltd.
Editorial Director: Lindsey Lowe
Managing Editor: Tim Cooke
Creative Director: Jeni Child
Picture Manager: Sophie Mortimer
Children's Publisher: Anne O'Daly

Library of Congress Cataloguing-in-Publication Data
available upon request

ISBN 978–1–936333–25–7

Printed in China

Picture credits

Front Cover: Library of Congress r; **Robert
Hunt Library** l

Corbis: 6, 10b, 26b, 31, 35, 38, 39; **Bettmann** 9b,
10t; 12b, 17, 21, 26t, 27, 29b, 30, 32, 34, 36b; **Edifice**
33t; **Hulton-Deutsch** 13, 15t, 18b, 20, 22, 23t, 36t;
iStock: 14; **Library of Congress**: 8, 9t, 11, 15b,
16, 24, 25; **Randall Bytwerk**: 12t; **Robert Hunt
Library**: 5, 7, 18t, 19, 23b, 28, 29t, 37;
Shutterstock: 33b

(Key: t = top, m = middle, b = bottom, l = left, r =
right)

Contents

Introduction

World War II was fought on fronts far from the battlefield. Civilians prepared to face bombing and its aftermath. Secret agents gathered information in the shadows. Codebreakers puzzled over enemy ciphers.

National security during wartime can be defined as including anything that helps protect the state and its citizens. That includes protection from both physical attack—invasion, sabotage, or bombing—and from attacks that threaten morale or political stability or espionage attempts to learn information that can benefit the enemy.

Threat from the Air

World War II was the first major conflict in which civilian populations came under bombardment from enemy aircraft on a large scale. Cities in Britain, Germany, and, later in the war, Japan were targeted by raids that involved hundreds of bombers.

Military planners believed that it was virtually impossible to prevent bombing raids, so they planned instead to deal with their effects. That involved providing shelters for civilians and firefighting, medical, and rescue teams. These often relied on volunteers, who also took responsibility for organizing public health services and even day-care for children.

Gaining Information

Modern warfare depends on information. Knowledge of the enemy's military plans is only one part of the overall picture. An understanding of public opinion might reveal low morale that can be exploited. Forewarning about the movements of leading personalities might offer a chance for assassination. Gossip about a change in working hours or machines in a factory might give clues about an enemy's change in weaponry or tactics and enable fighting forces to defend themselves against new threats.

Nations worked hard to limit the information that might reach the enemy. They also used espionage themselves. Spying took great courage—it was usually punished with death—but many secret agents went behind enemy lines to learn information or to perform acts of sabotage.

Code War

Military communications were routinely sent in code form by all sides in order to prevent the enemy from reading them. Throughout the military conflict a parallel struggle was fought between code setters and code breakers. As on the battlefield, the contest had both spectacular victories and tragic defeats.

⟹ **Posters like this image of a drowning U.S. sailor reinforced the link between the home front and the front line: the message was that everyone was equally responsible for national security.**

National Security

During wartime, life on the home front was shaped by the need to preserve national security, from civil defense measures to the censorship of correspondence.

 National security was a broad term. On the one hand, it included what is called "civil defense," a term that describes all nonmilitary actions taken during wartime to protect civilians and property from the effects of enemy action, such as, for example, air-raid precautions (see page 16). On the other hand, national security was a broader term that referred to anything that helped maintain the well-being of the nation, from keeping an eye on foreign citizens to ensuring that the media did not report any information that might be useful to the enemy. The president's wife, Eleanor Roosevelt, who helped establish the U.S. Office of Civilian Defense and acted as its chairwoman, argued that national defense depended on "better housing, better day-by-day medical care, better education, better nutrition for every age."

THE OFFICE OF CIVILIAN DEFENSE

The U.S. Office of Civilian Defense (OCD) was set up in May 1941. The committee set up air-raid precautions such as blackouts (in fact only a handful of bombs ever fell on U.S. soil; they were dropped by a Japanese seaplane in rural Oregon in 1942). The OCD ran the Civil Defense Corps, which trained about 10 million volunteers in firefighting, first aid, and other duties. Volunteer pilots of the Civil Air Patrol made look-out flights on the coasts.

ELEANOR ROOSEVELT

In February 1942 the First Lady resigned from the Office of Civilian Defense. Although she believed the OCD was essential, she thought her involvement subjected it to "political" attacks by enemies of her husband, the president.

⇐ **OCD chairwoman Eleanor Roosevelt encouraged community programs in order to help maintain public health and social welfare.**

'SPOT AT SIGHT' CHART Nº 1

ENEMY UNIFORMS

GERMAN PARACHUTIST

GERMAN SOLDIER

⇐ This poster was intended to help British civilians identify the enemy in the event of a German invasion.

Civilian Life

Ordinary people found their lives dominated by concerns related to national security. Most countries made citizens register and carry identity cards at all times, to make it easier to detect enemy agents. Propaganda was everywhere. There was an emphasis on good health and good nutrition: the more sickness there was at home, the more medicines, doctors, and nurses would have to be diverted from looking after front-line fighting forces. The American Office of Civilian Defense recruited female volunteers to provide day-care services so that women could go out to work.

There were frequent blackouts and curfews, which meant that people could not go outside their homes at night, unless they were on official duty. Even in the United States, blackouts were applied on the east and Gulf coasts. It was feared that lights on shore would illuminate coastal shipping and make it an easier target for U-boats lurking just out to sea.

> *This is the people's war. It is our war. We are the fighters!*
>
> MRS. MINIVER (FILM, 1942)

Enemy Aliens

All sides viewed enemy civilians (aliens) with suspicion. These were non-combatants—mainly women and children —from enemy nations who happened to be in a country when hostilities began or who were captured during an advance. The rapid Japanese advance through East Asia in December 1941, for example, left around 12,500 Allied civilians as prisoners, mostly in China and Hong Kong. They were herded into internment camps, where they were often subjected to harsh discipline, overcrowded conditions, and poor supplies of food.

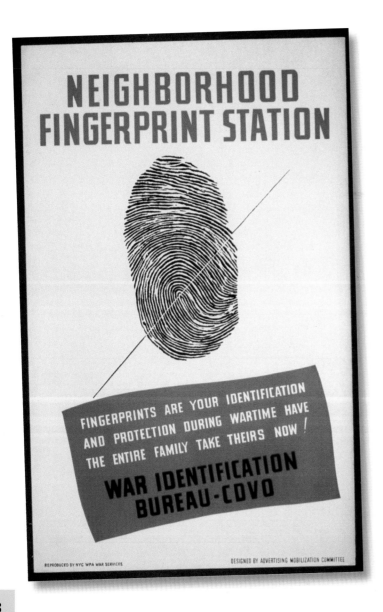

⇐ **This American poster stresses the need for citizens to have their fingerprints taken for purposes of identification. The war saw unprecedented levels of government monitoring of the population on all sides.**

In the United States, meanwhile, a concern for security after the Japanese attacks on Pearl Harbor in December 1941 created an atmosphere of suspicion about Japanese Americans. Japanese had lived on the West Coast since about 1885, and there was a long tradition of white Americans distrusting the Japanese.

Japanese Americans

About 110,000 Japanese Americans lived on the West Coast. It was feared that they might pass secrets on to the Japanese forces or help an enemy invasion through sabotage. In February 1942 President Franklin D. Roosevelt issued Executive Order 9066, which ordered that all Japanese Americans should be removed from coastal areas and sent inland.

⇐ This **OCD** poster calls for volunteers to help with a decontamination program run to improve public health by preventing sickness.

ZOOT SUIT RIOTS

Racial tension spilled over in Los Angeles in June 1943. Local Mexican youths had adopted a fashion for "zoot suits," with a long jacket and very baggy trousers. When it was reported that the "zoot suiters" had beaten up servicemen, white sailors from a nearby naval base rioted. They beat up anyone wearing zoot suits and stripped off their clothes. It took the police a few days to bring the situation under control.

⇒ Holding clubs, sailors and other servicemen look for Mexican youths in Los Angeles in June 1943.

Japanese Americans were originally free to emigrate to the East Coast, but only if they paid the cost of their own relocation. At the same time, the government limited how much money Japanese Americans could remove from their bank accounts. That made emigration impossible for most people to afford. In March 1942, all travel permits were cancelled, and internment became the only option. Some of the 10 hastily-built internment camps were in California, relatively close to the internees' former homes, but others were as far inland as Arkansas.

The camps were isolated—often in desert regions—and had only basic accommodation in wooden barracks. They were surrounded by barbed wire with guard towers.

Japanese Americans resented their internment. They were U.S. citizens, many of whom had never even been to Japan. They had built up businesses and purchased homes—both of which they were now forced to sell for virtually nothing. They ran the camps as small towns, with newspapers and schools; some camps even started the day with a ceremony that including singing the U.S.

⇒ Japanese American boy scouts and American Legionnaires hold a Memorial Day service at Manzanar Relocation Camp in California in 1942. Despite the prejudice of many whites (above), most Japanese Americans were loyal citizens.

national anthem. But they had few comforts—they were even forced to get rid of their pets.

The Home Guard

A number of countries began a kind of home guard. These units were intended to help defend the country against possible invasion. They were part of the regular army, but were not expected to perform front-line service.

In Britain, the Local Defence Volunteers (LDV) were created in May 1940, at a time when Prime Minister Winston Churchill believed that the country faced an imminent danger of German invasion. Churchill broadcast an appeal for volunteers and soon had 250,000 recruits. In August 1940 the name was changed (partly because the LDV had been nicknamed "Look, Duck, Vanish") to the Home Guard.

For most of the war about a million volunteers served in the Home Guard.

⇑ This U.S. poster reminds its audience that national security starts at home— maintaining public health by preventing the spread of diseases carried by flies.

ALIEN REGISTRATION ACT

In 1940 the U.S. government introduced the Alien Registration Act, sometimes also known as the Smith Act. The act made it a crime to publish material or make speeches calling for the overthrow of the U.S. government. It was intended to limit political criticism during wartime. It also made it compulsory for non-citizens to register with the government: up to 4.7 million adults registered within a few months. The act was used on two major occasions in World War II. In 1941 members of the communist Socialist Workers Party in Minneapolis were found guilty of remarking that U.S. servicemen should complain about their conditions of service. In 1944, in the "Great Sedition Trial," allegedly pro-fascist Americans were charged with arguing that the United States should not be involved in the war. The trial fell apart, however, because of lack of evidence. The act was always controversial because it contradicted the constitutional right to freedom of speech; it was last used in 1957, although it remains a law of the land.

⇒ **"For Freedom and Life" boasts this recruiting poster for the Volkssturm from autumn 1944. The armband was sometimes the only equipment a recruit received.**

Often they were too old to serve in the regular army or their jobs exempted them from military service.

The German invasion never came, however, so the Home Guard was never called on to fight. They helped patrol the coast and around 140,000 served in anti-aircraft units. Their main contribution was in freeing up regular armed forces for fighting overseas by covering many of the army's tasks on the home front.

The Volkssturm

In Germany, meanwhile, the equivalent of the Home Guard were the Volkssturm. They were formed in September 1944, as Germany's position became increasingly desperate. So many men had been killed, wounded, or captured that the Germans needed to recruit all the men they could. Already it was apparent that eventually the country was likely to be sandwiched between a Soviet advance from the east and an Allied advance from the west.

The German home-defense force was made up of men who were either too old to be in the army or teenagers who were too young to go to war. Many of the latter had been members of the Hitler Youth

⇐ **Wearing oversized uniforms, these 15- and 16-year-old Volkssturm recruits surrendered to the Americans during the Allied advance into Germany in April 1945.**

and were ideologically committed Nazis. About 6.2 million men were eligible to be drafted, although the total recruited was lower. The Volkssturm were usually poorly trained and had few weapons and low supplies of ammunition. Many had no uniforms, although they were all issued with arm bands that identified them as members of the force.

The Volkssturm made very little impact on the overall course of the war: Germany's defeat was, by the end of 1944, inevitable. But it did play a significant part in the final Battle of Berlin. It made up a large part of the 90,000 defenders of the German capital.

⇓ **Members of a Home Guard unit formed by employees of the General Post Office practice bayonet drill in London in 1941.**

> *Defend the homeland with all the weapons and means that seem appropriate.*
>
> ADOLF HITLER ORDERS TO VOLKSSTURM

DAD'S ARMY

Britain's Home Guard was affectionately known as Dad's Army (the name was later also used for a famous British TV comedy show about a Home Guard unit). It had a reputation as being slightly ineffectual. This was partly because, when it was originally formed, the units did not even have rifles. They practiced drill using broomsticks or shovels. The British playwright and composer Noel Coward wrote a comedy song about the shortages, entitled "Could You Please Oblige Us With a Bren Gun?" To begin with, the Home Guard was intended mainly to act as lookout, making patrols to observe any suspicious activity. Soon, however, its members were also trained in armed combat so that if necessary they could help to defend the country against a possible German invasion.

Some members of the Volkssturm fought bravely, especially after Goebbels' order on the radio that "Any man found not doing his duty will be hanged from a lamp post after a summary judgment."

Nevertheless, many Volkssturm elsewhere were eager to surrender to the Allies. Some of the younger members were barely more than children.

Censorship

One of the most important ways to protect national security was to limit the flow of information. This involved censorship, not just of the media but also of personal correspondence. In the United States, for example, one of those who fell foul of the official censor was the president's wife, Eleanor Roosevelt. The First Lady wrote a regular column that was printed in newspapers across the country. She was reprimanded in August 1942 for reporting on the weather while she was on a trip around the country with

⇑ **Pre-printed postcards allowed servicemen to communicate with their families without giving away vital information to the enemy.**

her husband. The censor believed that it might help the enemy work out where the president had been. Such scraps of information might betray where a new factory had opened or where an important meeting had taken place.

The United States created the Office of Censorship, led by Byron Price, a former news editor, in January 1942. Both Roosevelt and Price felt that censorship in World War I had gone too far. They were determined that any new code would be voluntary; all major news organizations agreed to take part.

In Germany, Japan, and the Soviet Union, meanwhile, the media had been heavily controlled by the government for years before the war broke out. They provided little reliable information about the progress of the conflict, although some Axis troops and civilians in Europe were able to get information from the British Broadcasting Corporation (BBC) and other broadcasters. When Soviet

CENSORSHIP

Even in western democracies, censorship was not entirely voluntary. In Britain, for example, the communist newspaper **The Daily Worker** *was banned altogether in 1941 for its opposition to the war. Newspapers were not allowed to print photographs that would damage morale, such as images of dead children. Some stories were kept secret for the same reason. Few civilians, for example, knew that the Japanese had begun making kamikaze attacks on Allied ships. On the other hand, the BBC was left to censor itself—which it did largely successfully. Sometimes the government simply did not give out any information to the media, or, if it did, deliberately gave false information.*

⟹ **The censor was empowered to simply return a message to the sender if the contents did not conform to the guidelines of what were permissible subjects for correspondence.**

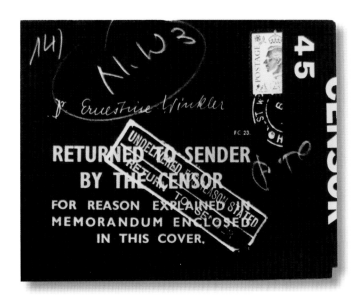

forces reached the German province of East Prussia in 1945, for example, they caused panic among a population who had been unaware of the enemy advance.

Personal correspondence was censored in virtually all combatant countries. The UK censorship office employed some 10,000 people; in the United States, the total was closer to 15,000. Censors were empowered to open and read mail in order to delete any information—usually about locations, conditions of service, or levels of supply—that might be useful to the enemy. Censors were also empowered simply to refuse to allow a letter to be sent through the post.

Soldiers, sailors, and others who were away on active service were often provided with pre-written postcards that simply allowed them to tick statements such as "I am safe and well." These were intended to reassure their families at home while at the same time not revealing even the smallest piece of information about their location or what they were doing.

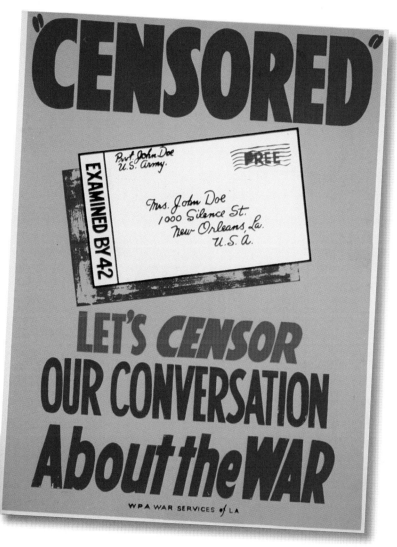

⟸ **As this U.S. poster underlines, censorship was not purely about written communication. Civilians were encouraged not to talk openly about anything to do with the war effort, such as their jobs in factories.**

Civil Defense

Civil defense describes all non-military actions that a country took to lessen the effects of enemy attacks. It usually depended on a large number of civilian volunteers.

Civil defense measures included the provision of air-raid shelters and drills to protect people from bombing raids; precautions against other forms of attack, such as the distribution of gas masks; the introduction of blackouts so that lights could not guide enemy pilots at night; and training civilians to act as firefighters or first aiders or to perform rescue tasks in the aftermath of an attack.

Threat from the Air

World War II was the first major conflict that involved large-scale aerial bombing of civilian targets behind enemy lines, so a key element of civil defense was taking precautions against air raids.

AERIAL BOMBING

World War II was the first time bombing was used on a large scale, but not the first time bombs had been dropped on civilians. In World War I German Zeppelins had dropped bombs on British cities, including London. The British press was outraged by the new form of aerial warfare.

ISSUED BY THE OAKLAND DEFENSE COUNCIL
WPA ART PROGRAM

THE BLACKOUT

The blackout aimed to prevent night bombers from finding their way by following lights on the ground. Homes and businesses had heavy curtains that allowed no light to escape. Street lights were switched off. Any vehicles that moved had only dim lights. One consequence of the blackout was a rise in traffic accidents; another was a rise in burglaries.

⇐ **This blackout poster was printed in the United States, but all countries that were subject to bombing raids used blackout tactics.**

⇒ **This image of St. Paul's Cathedral rising above smoke during an air raid became a famous symbol of London's enduring spirit during the Blitz.**

German aircraft during the Spanish Civil War pushed the British government's estimates even higher. However, it was widely condemned for predicting a million casualties in the first month of the war. Critics thought that such a figure would panic people unnecessarily.

As it turned out, bombing would cause more damage to property than to humans. Nevertheless, in the 12 months that followed the start of the Blitz in September 1940, more British civilians were killed than military personnel.

London Under Attack

The worst-hit target was London, the capital. From September 7 to November 2, 1940, the city was bombed every night during what was known as the "Blitz." The main targets were the docks in the

⟹ **The British government feared that the Germans would drop poison gas, so they issued gas masks to every citizen.**

In Britain, planners had studied the possible impact of bombing on the civilian population. There had been limited air attacks in World War I, and during the 1920s military strategists had been ruled by the idea that "the bomber will always get through."

On the basis that it was not possible to stop bombers, the authorities had to be prepared to deal with large numbers of casualties, particularly in London and other industrial cities. As World War II approached, however, estimates of the possible number of casualties rose alarmingly. The devastating bombing of the Basque town of Guernica in 1937 by

⟹ **In Britain drills were held in schools and workplaces so that people were accustomed to putting on and wearing their gas masks.**

THE BLITZ

In August 1940, frustrated at the failure of his plans to invade Britain, Adolf Hitler told the Luftwaffe to focus on bombing London and other cities. This Blitz—short for "Blitzkrieg," or "lightning war"—began on September 7. For the first month or so, London was bombed every night. The capital had only 92 anti-aircraft guns, which could not offer much defense. In mid-November the Blitz spread to industrial centers including Coventry, Sheffield, and Birmingham and to ports such as Portsmouth and Swansea. The Blitz tailed off in May 1941, as the Germans prepared to invade the Soviet Union, although air raids continued into 1944. More than 60,000 civilians had died, but morale was not destroyed. The "spirit of the Blitz" became part of the way the British saw themselves and their resilience.

⇒ **Emergency rest centers were set up in churches, schools, and cinemas to provide shelter for people who had lost their homes in the Blitz.**

East End of the city, which were surrounded by dense housing. Incendiary bombs did most damage by setting fire to property. Some 3.5 million homes were damaged. Other buildings that suffered were landmarks such as Buckingham Palace and the Houses of Parliament. After one night of air raids in the town of Clydebank in Scotland, a target because of its many shipyards, only seven houses were left undamaged.

As part of civil defense procedures, the government had set up plans for the evacuation of children from Britain's cities. The major evacuation—1.5 million children—took place in a few days in September 1939, at the start of the war, and went remarkably smoothly. When no German bombing came initially, many of the evacuees moved back home. However, after the Blitz began in 1940, more than a million people fled the cities again to safer places in the countryside.

Air Raid Precautions

Air-raid precautions—known as ARP—had been increased as British government predictions of casualties rose before the war began. In the first year of the war government spending on ARP, which was already relatively high, increased by nearly threefold.

London buses drive through a smoke screen. This was part of an exercise in 1942 that simulated an attack on Westminster.

ARP such as rescue or first-aid duties were initially largely the responsibility of volunteers. In July 1940 the government froze the voluntary ARP services. That meant that no volunteers were allowed to leave. In January 1941, new legislation required firms to provide a list of employees who would stand watch during the night. Based on rooftops, these fire spotters looked out for flames that marked a blaze begun by bombs. ARP volunteers were trained in firefighting.

GAS MASKS

The British government believed that the Germans might use poison gas against civilian populations. The Germans had pioneered the use of gas on the Western Front during World War I (1914–1918). The British issued gas masks to all civilians (including gas cots for babies). The masks were placed over the head and strapped in place. They had a close-fitting facepiece that formed an air-tight seal around the face. The protrusion at the front of the gas mask contained a carbon filter designed to let in air but block out the particulates of poison.

Taking Cover

In the case of an approaching air raid, warning sirens sounded in Britain's cities. They gave people enough notice to take shelter. Householders with gardens were able to take cover in an Anderson shelter. Named after the government official who introduced them, Anderson shelters were made from a tunnel of corrugated iron that was partly buried in the ground. Sleeping up to six people, the shelters were given away free to the poor and sold cheaply to others: some 1.5 million shelters were put up before the war began, and more than 2 million after.

Anderson shelters offered good protection from blasts—other than a direct hit—but they were cold and damp. In spring 1941 indoor Morrison shelters were introduced: low cages made from steel frames with wire sides. By then, the worst of the bombing had passed.

The Subway

In London, many people took shelter at night in any buildings that had a cellar (including at least one funeral home with a basement morgue). A favorite shelter was the subway station. Londoners slept on the platforms to avoid night bombings. The government had tried to ban the practice, partly because of worries about sanitation and partly because it was concerned that people would be reluctant to leave the shelters to go to work. But Londoners ignored the ban. Up to 177,000 people slept in the stations, so the authorities provided toilets and camp beds. However, even during the worst nights of the Blitz, more than half of Londoners—six out of ten—continued to sleep at home.

Eyewitness
IVY OATES

British student Ivy Oates took cover with another woman at New Street Station in Birmingham.

"The sirens went and the lady said to me 'We have to go down the luggage subway.' We went underground, to a dark musty passage. Suddenly, she grabbed me and shouted, 'A rat! A rat!' I'd rather have an air raid than a rat. So we went back on the platform."

⇐ Londoners bed down for the night in a subway station during the Blitz.

New Threats

The height of the Blitz was over by late 1940. By then, there had been massive and widespread destruction of property. The fighters of the Royal Air Force, however, had defeated the Luftwaffe's attempt to bomb Britain into surrender. Later in the war, the threat to British civilians would come from new weapons: the flying bombs. The V-1 and the V-2 were long-range rockets that could be fired from northern France at London. The V-1 was nicknamed the Doodlebug because of the high-pitched sound of its engine. Some 9,500 V-1s were fired at southern England between June 1944 and October, when Allied soldiers captured the last launch site. The Germans then targeted the V-1 on Belgian cities while they fired V-2 rockets at Britain from bases further away.

66 *The night it started, it looked as if the whole of London was burning.*

LIL MURRELL ON THE START OF THE BLITZ 99

Allied Bombing Campaign

The Allies began to bomb industrial targets in Germany early in the war. By 1942, they switched to raids that aimed to undermine enemy morale by destroying larger areas. An RAF directive ordered

⇒ **British sailors learn to identify aircraft from models hanging on a clothes line in 1940.**

that "the only target on which the night force could inflict effective damage was a whole German town."

German air defense relied on a network of searchlights and anti-aircraft guns along the North Sea coast from Denmark to Belgium, with other dense defenses around Berlin and the Ruhr industrial region. The Allies were able to overcome the defenses—but frequently at a huge cost in aircraft. In 1942 Bomber Command sent 1,047 aircraft on a night-time raid on Cologne. In February 1945

⇑ **A British aircraft-spotter uses binoculars and a specially adapted chair to check the skies for enemy airplanes at a training camp in 1939.**

four raids on Dresden started firestorms that destroyed about 15 square miles (39 square kilometers) of the city. Up to 25,000 people died in the attack.

Fire also destroyed much of the Japanese capital, Tokyo, in raids in March 1945. Once U.S. forces got within range, long-distance B-29 bombers attacked Japanese cities frequently (the Japanese had few defenses by then). A 335-bomber raid on Tokyo on the night of March 9, 1945, started a firestorm that killed up to 100,000 people (and possibly even more)—a higher immediate death toll than the atomic bombs that ended the war a few months later.

A·R·P

here's a *man's* job!

⇐ **The British campaign to recruit ARP wardens was highly successful. By the time war broke out in 1939, there were 1.5 million wardens. Despite the claim that it was a "man's job," the wardens included many women.**

Spies and Spying

Espionage is an important part of warfare. Any information about the enemy might be useful in gaining an advantage on the battlefield. But spying has always been a dangerous game.

Spies were everywhere. No one ever knew what piece of information might prove useful to the enemy. Secret services recruited agents in enemy countries, or sent them in. There was also a lot of espionage activity in neutral countries such as Spain, where citizens of all combatant countries could mingle freely.

Intelligence Networks

At the start of the war, the German intelligence service, the Abwehr, already had agents in useful positions. The head of the service, Wilhelm Canaris, had made sure that his agents were prepared for the coming conflict. His Duquesne spy ring in the United States had more than 30 agents. They smuggled information back to Germany in microdots only 1 millimeter across.

⇒ **Authorities were worried about information being passed to the enemy, although it was actually a rare occurrence. This U.S. poster brought home the potential results of a breech of security.**

⇧ This poster underlined that it was a patriotic duty of Americans not to discuss anything about the war effort that might be useful to spies.

SPY GADGETS

The need to equip wartime agents inspired the creation of some remarkable gadgets, such as micro-cameras that were concealed in cigarette lighters. Microdots were tiny photographs disguised as full-stops in written messages. Shoes were adapted to hide knives and saws. Shaving brushes could conceal rolls of film. Tiny needles could be magnetized and inserted inside matchsticks, which would indicate north if they were dropped into water. Codes and escape maps were hidden inside playing cards, which could be dampened and peeled apart in layers. There were maps printed on handkerchiefs using invisible ink. The Germans even created a grenade that was disguised as a bar of chocolate.

ANTON OTTO FISCHER

a careless word...

A NEEDLESS LOSS

OWI Poster No. 36.   Additional copies may be obtained upon request from the Division of Public Inquiries, Office of War Information, Washington, D. C.   U S GOVERNMENT PRINTING OFFICE 1943 O 506018

 A federal agent displays weapons, signal equipment, and other material captured from Nazi sympathizers in upstate New York in 1942. There was a real fear that enemy aliens might help foreign agents.

obtain plans of all of the forts and fortifications defending the eastern border of France. In Turkey, an agent who had a job as a servant to the British ambassador was able to pass many secrets on to Germany. In Poland, agents misled the Poles with information that made it easier for German invaders to conquer the country in September 1939.

Spies in the United States

As the war went on, German spies continued to plan active operations. In May 1942 in Operation Pastorius, two U-boats sailed to the United States and dropped off eight German agents. Four landed on Long Island in New York, while another four landed on a beach in

Messages were photographed and then shrunk so small they could be hidden virtually anywhere. The Americans were astonished when they intercepted their first microdot in 1941.

A German agent in France had a job at a cement factory that allowed him to

WARNING
from the
FBI

The war against spies and saboteurs demands the aid of every American.

When you see evidence of sabotage, notify the Federal Bureau of Investigation at once.

When you suspect the presence of enemy agents, tell it to the FBI.

Beware of those who spread enemy propaganda! <u>Don't repeat vicious rumors or vicious whispers.</u>

Tell it to the FBI!

J. Edgar Hoover, Director
Federal Bureau of Investigation

The nearest Federal Bureau of Investigation office is listed on page one of your telephone directory.

ESPIONAGE IN THE UNITED STATES

German efforts to spy in the Americas had mixed results. Attempts at sabotage in May 1942 ended with the capture of eight agents soon after they landed in the United States. Another agent was arrested at a hotel in Canada, where he aroused suspicion by having a matchbox from a bar in Brussels, Belgium. In Latin America, however, German agents ran spy networks in Brazil, Chile, and Argentina. Before the United States entered the war in late 1941, these agents gathered useful information from U.S. documents about British ship movements and industrial output. The Allies later pressured the governments of those countries to shut down the spy rings.

arrested, tried, and executed (the two defectors received prison sentences, but returned to Germany after the war).

Secret Services

Both the British and the Americans set up organizations to coordinate the efforts of agents in enemy territory. The British set up the Special Operations Executive (SOE) while the U.S. equivalent was the Office of Strategic Services (OSS). The SOE specialized in subversion. It used espionage and sabotage to destabilize Axis forces. It operated by recruiting agents that it trained to blow up railroad lines or factories or to blend in with the local population while they gathered information. Individuals with language skills were the best recruits, who included 3,000 women: women aroused less suspicion and coped better with the permanent stress of being an agent.

⇓ **This matchbox camera produced by the Eastman Kodak company allowed OSS agents to take secret photographs.**

SPECIAL OPERATIONS EXECUTIVE

The British set up the Special Operations Executive (SOE) in 1940 by combining three secret service organizations. Its purpose was to coordinate propaganda and sabotage efforts in enemy territory. The SOE sent hundreds of agents into European countries. They used inventions like limpet mines to destroy property or transportation links. They also advised resistance movements. The SOE chief cryptographer, Leo Marks, came up with one-off codes that agents could use for wireless communications with the SOE.

Florida. The agents had received training in explosives and were on a mission to sabotage power plants and factories, along with Jewish businesses. They had fake biographies to use as cover stories.

In fact, the agents on Long Island were spotted by a coastguard as soon as they came ashore. They offered him a bribe to keep quiet, but he reported them to his supervisors anyway (although he did take the bribe). The FBI launched a manhunt but in the meantime two of the agents lost their nerve. They decided to defect to the Americans and turned themselves in. The police were reluctant to believe them, but were eventually convinced. The two men reported the locations of the other agents, who were

The OSS also carried out sabotage and espionage missions, as well as training Yugoslavian partisans to fight the Germans and training German refugees to spy inside Germany.

Helping the Resistance

Both the SOE and the OSS worked closely with resistance movements in occupied countries. The OSS helped train guerrillas in Southeast Asia, for example, while the SOE supplied more than 500,000 weapons to the French Resistance during the run-up to D-Day in June 1944. They used Lysander aircraft, which could land on fields at night and only needed 110 yards (100 meters) to take off or land; Lysanders flew more than 800 missions from 1941 to 1944.

Among the many agents the SOE dropped into France was Violette Szabo, who helped organize a Resistance unit and sabotage German transportation. When she was captured, Szabo was tortured—which was common for captured spies—but she did not betray her contacts in the Resistance. She finally was sent to a concentration camp, where she was eventually executed aged just 23.

"..... but of course it *mustn't* go *any* further!"

CARELESS TALK COSTS LIVES

⇑ **British cartoonist Cyril Kenneth Bird produced a whole series of posters that show senior Nazis listening in as people carelessly give away war secrets.**

Eyewitness

ERWIN VON LAHOUSEN

Austrian Von Lahousen was deputy to Wilhelm Canaris, head of the Abwehr.

"Canaris was a personality of pure intellect. We relied on his inner very unique and complicated nature for this reason. He hated violence and therefore hated Hitler, his abominable system, and particularly his methods. Canaris was ... a human being."

⇐ **"Keep your lips silent" reads this Japanese poster. Factory police enforced discipline in every Japanese war plant.**

In 1944 Skorzeny began Operation Greif to counter the American advance in the Ardennes. The plan was that Skorzeny would lead a unit of SS men disguised in British and U.S. uniforms. They would attempt to capture a bridge and cause disruption behind enemy lines. The operation failed and some of Skorzeny's agents were captured and executed by the Americans (wearing enemy uniform marked someone as a spy and was a capital offense). Skorzeny himself escaped. He went on to become a spy in Latin America after the war. According to some accounts, he may have helped smuggle senior Nazis to new lives in the Americas.

Skorzeny the Spy

The German Waffen SS officer Otto Skorzeny became renowned in 1943 for leading the operation that rescued the Italian dictator, Benito Mussolini, when he was imprisoned by the Allies. Skorzeny had also kidnapped the son of the Hungarian prime minister and forced the prime minister to resign in favor of a more pro-Hitler government.

⇒ **U.S. military police tie a German agent to a post before his execution by firing squad for spying on troop and supply movements behind Allied lines in spring 1945.**

Codes and Code Breaking

CODE ANALYSIS

Although the British pioneered the use of computers to decipher codes, most code-breaking relied on people. Mathematicians and puzzle enthusiasts spent hours poring over coded messages. They used alphabet strips and other tools to search for hidden patterns behind the code. They also used basic facts to form the basis for a decryption, such as how often a letter occurs in a language. The work was often done in great secrecy: some cryptologists could not even tell their families about their work.

⇓ **An analyst uses alphabet strips to try to work out any underlying patterns that might help reveal a code's meaning.**

During World War II, security was vitally important, even on the home front. People were warned to think carefully about what they revealed in careless chatter.

The need to keep communications secret led to great advances in codes and ciphers (a code is any set of symbols or signs with hidden meanings; a cipher is a code that substitutes individual symbols or letters). What made maintaining secrecy more difficult was that the most common means of long-distance communication —radio—allowed the enemy to eavesdrop on what was being said.

Codes could vary from the relatively simple to highly complex codes generated by machines, and sometimes these were used only once by agents before being discarded.

The Enigma Machine

The Germans had adopted a complex coding machine in the late 1920s. Named Enigma, the device looked like a small wooden box with a keyboard that resembled that of a typewriter.

⇒ **German soldiers in the field send a message on an Enigma machine. The rotors of the machine, which were set in different positions each day, generated millions of possible combinations.**

It had a series of rotors beneath the keys that rotated to turn a written message into what appeared to be a random series of numbers. The settings of the rotors changed every day, so Allied codebreakers were always trying to decipher a cipher that had already been changed by the Germans.

The different services had different codes. The secrets of the German Navy were the most secure; the least secure were those of the Luftwaffe, or air force. In 1941, for example, when the Royal Navy was searching for the German battleship *Bismarck*, it could not decipher the codes from the ship. But a senior official in the Luftwaffe had a son onboard and he signaled Berlin to find out where the ship was. The British were able to decipher the Luftwaffe reply and track the ship. They eventually sank it in the Atlantic Ocean about 350 miles (560 kilometers) west of Brittany in France.

Cracking the Enigma

The British knew how Enigma worked, however. Their Polish allies had shown them a copy of an Enigma machine shortly before the war began. The British also built an early model of a computer—called Colossus—to help them process different permutations to crack the German codes. The process was not easy and still took time: usually too long for the decoded messages to be useful. But then in March 1941 a naval boarding party in the Atlantic went on board the captured submarine *U-110* and found a German naval Enigma machine.

By the summer of 1941 the British could regularly read German U-boat signals—sometimes within only a few hours. That continued until, in February 1942, the Germans introduced a new level of complications to their codes that prevented any deciphering until December. It still took six months or so

WIND TALKERS

In the Pacific U.S. forces were able to send secret radio signals in a code that the Japanese simply could not understand. The code was based on the Native American Navajo language, which was so complex that only about 30 non-Navajo spoke it. Some 400 Navajo volunteers learned the code and served as radio operators during the Pacific campaign. They sent messages to one another that were quickly decoded, translated into English, and passed on. Native Americans had also been used to pass messages during World War I (1914–1918) and would be used again in northern Europe on D-Day.

⇩ **A two-man team of Navajo code talkers send radio messages in the field in the Pacific; Navajo had no written version, making it an ideal code.**

BLETCHLEY PARK

The British code-breaking effort was based at the top-secret "Station X," a manor house north of London named Bletchley Park. The British gathered a team of scientists, mathematicians, and academics—but also people who enjoyed crosswords and number puzzles. Station X was top secret—the codebreakers who worked there could not even tell their families what they were working on. The team was broken into "huts," which each tackled a particular part of the stream of coded messages that the Allies gathered every day. Hut 8, led by the mathematician Alan Turing, was responsible for tackling German naval codes. To help them, Turing oversaw the construction of one of the earliest of all computers, known as Colossus. The breakthrough came in summer 1941, when the Allies captured a book of German code settings.

⇑ The huts at Bletchley Park were preserved after the war as a memorial to the remarkable work done there in deciphering signals sent by the Enigma machine (left).

to be able to crack the new codes consistently. Once the Allies had managed that, however, in summer 1943, they continued to read German signals easily until the end of the war.

Confidence in Codes

The Germans had no idea until after the war how fully their secret codes had been broken. The Germans assumed that the British seemed to know so much about their U-boat operations from the Allies' development of radar, not from having broken the German codes. Like the Germans, meanwhile, the Japanese believed that their codes were more secure than they proved to be. Even after the war, some Japanese cryptologists still refused to believe that their Purple code had been broken by using code analysis alone. They insisted—wrongly—that informers must have passed on details about the codes to the Americans.

RADAR

Early in the war British and American scientists developed radar - (RA)dio (D)etection (A)nd (R)anging - as a way to locate objects using radio waves.

66 *The geese that laid the golden egg—*
but never cackled.

WINSTON CHURCHILL ON BLETCHLEY PARK

Axis Code Breaking

The Allies were not the only side that successfully broke enemy codes. Early in the war, the Germans found it relatively straightforward to decipher all but the highest level British naval signals. The Royal Navy relied on manual coding systems rather than machines like Enigma. The British improved their system in 1940, but by late 1941 the German code breakers again had the upper hand. It was only from their own efforts at decoding German messages that the British realized they still had to improve their own system. In the summer of 1943 the British finally upgraded it to a more secure level.

Eyewitness

PATRICIA BROWN

Brown worked as a code breaker at Bletchley Park in Britain.

"I remember only one small triumph. We were working with five-figure subtraction ciphers, where it was necessary to subtract one group from another to get at the result which could, with luck, be decoded. I noticed some regularities that no one else had seen, which vastly reduced the number of groups that needed to be decoded. I never knew the lasting significance."

The Japanese Purple code was generated by a machine the Japanese called Alphabetic Typewriter 97. The U.S. Army Signals Intelligence Service (SIS) assumed it was a rotor machine, like Enigma. After months of failed analysis, however, William Friedman of the SIS realized that the machine worked not by using rotors but electrical switches, as telephone exchanges worked at the time. The Americans soon built what later turned out to be an almost exact replica of the Japanese machine.

The breakthrough not only allowed the Americans to follow Japanese plans

DEATH OF YAMAMOTO

Admiral Isoroku Yamamoto was the commander in chief of Japan's Combined Fleet. At the start of the war he had been responsible for planning the attack on the U.S. naval base at Pearl Harbor on December 7, 1941. Unknown to the Japanese, the U.S. "Magic" code-breaking operation had broken the Japanese Purple code. In spring 1943 U.S. cryptographers learned that Yamamoto would be flying from his headquarters to visit airfields being built on Bougainville in the northern Solomon Islands. President F. D. Roosevelt ordered the U.S. Navy to intercept him. On April 18, U.S. fighters attacked Yamamoto's aircraft, killing him. His death was a major blow to Japanese morale.

⇐ **Isoroku Yamamoto was commander in chief of the Japanese Combined Fleet. When President Roosevelt heard the intelligence about Yamamoto's movements, he ordered the Secretary of the Navy to "Get Yamamoto."**

in the Pacific—they could also read the messages of Japan's ambassador in Berlin, and so learn the secrets of Germany's Japanese allies.

The Japanese naval code JN-25b was not cracked until 1942. The Americans learned that the Japanese were planning an attack at a location encoded as AF. On a hunch, U.S. code breakers contacted Midway, a Pacific island used to refuel aircraft, and got the base there to transmit false messages that it was short of water. When Japanese signals reported that AF was short of water, the Americans had located the target. They rushed their fleet there, and the battle that followed in June 1942 was a U.S. victory and a turning point in the whole Pacific War.

Secrets and Deception

During World War II, security was vitally important, even on the home front. People were warned to think carefully about what they might reveal through careless chatter.

Spies could be anywhere, and information about troop movements, ship locations, or even what was being made in munitions factories might be invaluable to the enemy. People were warned to "Keep Mum" and that "Loose Lips Sink Ships."

Careless Talk

In February 1940 the Ministry of Information in Britain launched a campaign with the slogan "Careless Talk Costs Lives." Two and a half million posters were printed and displayed in offices, stores, factories, and bars. Some of the posters took a hard approach to make the public take notice.

⬆ **British reconnaissance experts examine a strip of images taken by a reconnaissance aircraft in 1944.**

⬅ **This aerial photograph, taken in June 1943, was the first to show the site at Peenemunde, Germany, from which V-2 rockets were launched at targets in Britain and Belgium; a rocket lies on its side at "A."**

⟹ **This British poster uses a simple presentation and direct wording to drive home the importance of its message.**

DON'T HELP THE ENEMY!

CARELESS TALK MAY GIVE AWAY VITAL SECRETS

Slogans such as "They Talked ... This Happened" drove home the message that unguarded comments could have severe consequences. The U.S. Office of War Information printed more posters that showed the result of careless talk: ships being sunk, trains being blown up, or the body of a sailor washed up on a beach.

Other countries ran similar campaigns. The basic messages were the same. Anyone could be an enemy spy, and any scrap of information might be useful to the enemy. It was better for everyone, whether or not they were involved in the war effort, to keep their mouths shut.

There were other ways to conceal information from the enemy. One was censorship. All nations censored the amount of detail that was published in newspapers, in case it revealed information to the enemy (in countries such as the United States, such censorship was voluntary). The British, meanwhile, tried to make sure that enemy agents would find it difficult to gather information by removing road signs and other signs that indicated the names of places. In the event, this precaution only served to disrupt British civilians who needed to visit places they didn't know.

RUDOLF HESS

One of the Allies' most unusual sources of information about Nazi Germany was Rudolf Hess, deputy leader of the Nazi Party. In May 1941 Hess stole an airplane and parachuted into Scotland. He believed he would be able to stop the war. Although the British thought he was suffering from depression—and was possibly mad—they carefully debriefed Hess to learn everything that they could about the German leadership. They were particularly interested, for example, in Adolf Hitler's interest in the occult.

⇑ **Rudolf Hess (seated, right) was tried at Nuremberg after the war and was sentenced to life imprisonment.**

Misinformation

An extension of keeping information from the enemy was to give the enemy false information. The Allies used wooden tanks to mislead German reconnaisance about their firepower. They also developed camouflage that would disguise tanks and other equipment from the air. When a German agent named Zigzag joined the British as a double agent, British intelligence faked Zigzag's planned raid on an armaments factory to make the Germans think that he had succeeded in his mission.

RECONNAISSANCE

In 1938 General Werner von Fritsch of the German High Command predicted that "The military organization with the best aerial reconnaissance will win the war." During the conflict, aircraft carrying high-resolution cameras flew hundreds of reconnaissance flights. Their images provided details that could be added to maps to help ground forces. They also kept a record of the damage caused by bombing raids and the effectiveness of enemy attempts to repair the damage after a raid.

⟹ **A U.S. Navy photographer fastens a reconnaissance camera to the cockpit of an airplane. At sea, aerial photographs made it possible to assess bomb damage to enemy vessels.**

The Man Who Never Was

One of the most celebrated stories of deception in the war was the "man who never was." Mincemeat was a British intelligence operation that involved the body of a drowned man. The British dressed the body in a major's uniform and gave it false papers that identified the dead man as William Martin. They chained a briefcase to the body's wrist containing plans for an Allied invasion of Greece and the Balkans.

The body of "Major Martin" was secretly taken by submarine to a destination near Spain, where it was released. When the body washed up on shore, German spies got hold of the documents. They checked out Major Martin and were convinced that he was genuine—so they assumed the plans were, too. The Germans ordered the Italian fleet guarding Sicily to head to Greece to prevent the Allied invasion—leaving the way open for the real Allied plan, which was actually to invade Sicily. That invasion went ahead with little resistance in July 1943.

FALSE PAPERS

To make sure the Germans believed Major Martin was real, the British faked letters from other army officers and included them with his orders. They even included ticket stubs for a London theater. At home, they announced his "death" in the newspaper.

Timeline of World War II

1939

SEPTEMBER:

German troops invade and overrun Poland

Britain and France declare war on Germany

The Soviet Union invades eastern Poland and extends control to the Baltic states

The Battle of the Atlantic begins

NOVEMBER:

The Soviet Union launches a winter offensive against Finland

1940

APRIL:

Germany invades Denmark and Norway

Allied troops land in Norway

MAY:

Germany invades Luxembourg, the Netherlands, Belgium, and France

Allied troops are evacuated at Dunkirk

JUNE:

Italy declares war on France and Britain

German troops enter Paris

France signs an armistice with Germany

Italy bombs Malta in the Mediterranean

JULY:

German U-boats inflict heavy losses on Allied convoys in the Atlantic

Britain sends warships to neutralize the French fleet in North Africa

The Battle of Britain begins

SEPTEMBER:

Luftwaffe air raids begin the Blitz—the bombing of London and other British cities

Italian troops advance from Libya into Egypt

Germany, Italy, and Japan sign the Tripartite Pact

OCTOBER:

Italy invades Greece; Greek forces, aided by the British, mount a counterattack

DECEMBER:

British troops at Sidi Barrani, Egypt, force the Italians to retreat

1941

JANUARY:

Allied units capture Tobruk in Libya

British forces in Sudan attack Italian East Africa

FEBRUARY:

Allies defeat Italy at Benghazi, Libya

Rommel's Afrika Korps arrive in Tripoli

MARCH:

The Africa Korps drive British troops back from El Agheila

APRIL:

German, Italian and Hungarian units invade Yugoslavia

German forces invade Greece

The Afrika Korps beseige Tobruk

MAY:

The British sink the German battleship *Bismarck*

JUNE:

German troops invade the Soviet Union

JULY:

German forces advance to within 10 miles (16 kilometers) of Kiev

AUGUST:

The United States bans the export of oil to Japan

SEPTEMBER:

German forces start the siege of Leningrad

German Army Group Center advances on Moscow

NOVEMBER:

British troops begin an attack to relieve Tobruk

The Allies liberate Ethiopia

DECEMBER:

Japanese aircraft attack the U.S. Pacific Fleet at Pearl Harbor

Japan declares war on the United States and Britain

The United States, Britain, and the Free French declare war on Japan

Japanese forces invade the Philippines, Malaya, and Thailand, and defeat the British garrison in Hong Kong

1942

JANUARY:

Japan attacks the Dutch East Indies and invades Burma

Rommel launches a new offensive in Libya

FEBRUARY:
Singapore surrenders to the Japanese
APRIL:
The Bataan Peninsula in the Philippines falls to the Japanese
MAY:
U.S. and Japanese fleets clash at the Battle of the Coral Sea
Rommel attacks the Gazala Line in Libya
JUNE:
The U.S. Navy defeats the Japanese at the Battle of Midway
Rommel recaptures Tobruk and the Allies retreat to Egypt
JULY:
The Germans take Sebastopol after a long siege and advance into the Caucasus
AUGUST:
U.S. Marines encounter fierce Japanese resistance in the Solomons
SEPTEMBER–OCTOBER:
Allied forces defeat Axis troops at El Alamein, Egypt—the first major Allied victory of the war
NOVEMBER:
U.S. and British troops land in Morocco and Algeria

1943

FEBRUARY:
The German Sixth Army surrenders at Stalingrad
The Japanese evacuate troops from Guadalcanal in the Solomons
MAY:
Axis forces in Tunisia surrender, ending the campaign in North Africa
JULY:
U.S. troops make landings on New Georgia Island in the Solomons
The Red Army wins the Battle of Kursk
Allied troops land on Sicily
British bombers conduct massive raids on Hamburg
AUGUST:
German forces occupy Italy
SEPTEMBER:
Allied units begin landings on mainland Italy
Italy surrenders, prompting a German invasion of northern Italy
OCTOBER:
The Red Army liberates the Caucasus
NOVEMBER:
U.S. carrier aircraft attack Rabaul in the Solomons

1944

JANUARY:
The German siege of Leningrad ends
FEBRUARY:
U.S. forces conquer the Marshall Islands

MARCH:
The Soviet offensive reaches the Dniester River
Allied aircraft bomb the monastery at Monte Cassino in Italy
JUNE:
U.S. troops enter the city of Rome
D-Day–the Allies begin the invasion of northern Europe
U.S. aircraft defeat the Japanese fleet at the Battle of the Philippine Sea
JULY:
The Red Army begins its offensive to clear the Baltic states
Soviet tanks enter Poland
AUGUST:
Japanese troops withdraw from Myitkyina in Burma
French forces liberate Paris
Allied units liberate towns in France, Belgium, and the Netherlands
OCTOBER:
Soviet and Yugoslavian troops capture Belgrade, the Yugoslav capital
The Japanese suffer defeat at the Battle of Leyte Gulf
DECEMBER:
Hitler counterattacks in the Ardennes in the Battle of the Bulge

1945

JANUARY:
The U.S. Army lands on Luzon in the Philippines
The Red Army liberates Auschwitz
Most of Poland and Czechoslovakia are liberated by the Allies
FEBRUARY:
U.S. troops take the Philippine capital, Manila
U.S. Marines land on the island of Iwo Jima
Soviet troops strike west across Germany
The U.S. Army heads towards the Rhine River
APRIL:
U.S. troops land on the island of Okinawa
Mussolini is shot by partisans
Soviet troops assault Berlin
Hitler commits suicide in his bunker
MAY:
All active German forces surrender
JUNE:
Japanese resistance ends in Burma and on Okinawa
AUGUST:
Atomic bombs are dropped on Hiroshima and Nagasaki
Japan surrenders

World War II: Europe

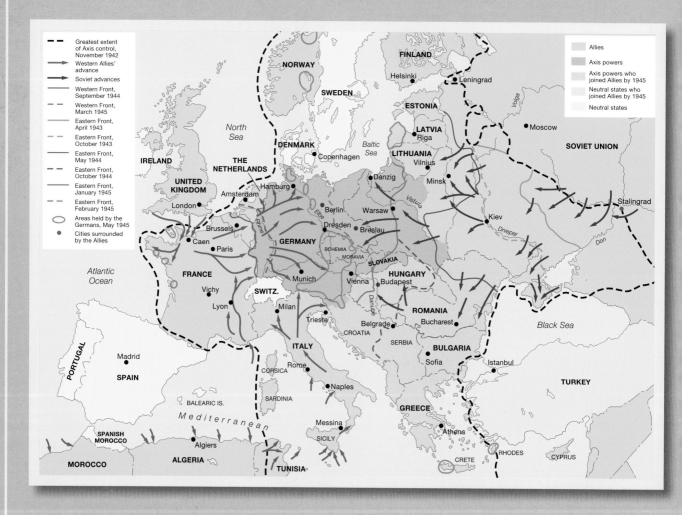

Greatest extent of Axis control, November 1942
Western Allies' advance
Soviet advances
Western Front, September 1944
Western Front, March 1945
Eastern Front, April 1943
Eastern Front, October 1943
Eastern Front, May 1944
Eastern Front, October 1944
Eastern Front, January 1945
Eastern Front, February 1945
Areas held by the Germans, May 1945
Cities surrounded by the Allies

Allies
Axis powers
Axis powers who joined Allies by 1945
Neutral states who joined Allies by 1945
Neutral states

The war began with rapid German advances through the Low Countries and northern France. In June 1941 German armies struck through eastern Europe into the Soviet Union, besieging Leningrad and Stalingrad. However, Allied landings in North Africa led to eventual victory there and opened the way for the invasion of Sicily and then of the Italian peninsula itself, forcing Italy to surrender. In the east the defeat of the German Sixth Army at Stalingrad forced a long retreat during which German forces were harried by communist guerrillas at all moments. In June 1944 Allied forces landed in northern France on D-Day and began to fight their way toward Berlin. As the Soviet advance closed in and the Americans and British crossed the Rhine River into Germany, defeat became inevitable. Hitler committed suicide in his bunker at the heart of his failed Reich, or empire.

World War II: The Pacific

The Pacific conflict began with swift Japanese advances in and occupation of territory throughout Southeast Asia, Malaya, the East Indies, the Philippines, and the island groups of the Pacific. The U.S. fleet was weakened by the attack on Pearl Harbor, but the damage it suffered was repaired remarkably quickly. After the naval victory at Midway in June 1942, U.S. commanders fought a campaign of "island hopping," overcoming strong local Japanese resistance to establish a series of stepping stones that would bring their bombers close enough to attack the Japanese home islands. Meanwhile, British and Indian troops pushed back the Japanese advance from Burma.

Biographies

Neville Chamberlain

British statesman. Conservative prime minister from 1937 to 1940, Chamberlain led the policy of appeasement of Hitler. He argued that giving in to Hitler's demands was the best way to prevent war. When the policy failed, he resigned in favor of Winston Churchill.

Churchill, Winston

British statesman. Churchill became British prime minister in May 1940 after a controversial political career. He was an energetic, inspiring, and imaginative leader. His powerful speeches and his cultivation of Britain's U.S. allies were vital to the Allies' war effort. After the war's end Churchill was defeated in a general election, but he became prime minister again in 1951.

De Gaulle, Charles

French statesman. French army officer De Gaulle escaped to London after the German invasion of France in 1939 and set up the Free French to oppose the Vichy regime's collaboration with Germany. Under De Gaulle's leadership, the Free French grew to include some 300,000 fighters, including partisans of the French Resistance. In 1945 he was elected president of France and later founded the Fifth French Republic.

Eisenhower, Dwight D.

U.S. general. Eisenhower was part of the U.S. war plans division when he was promoted in June 1942 to become commander of U.S. forces in Europe. He led the Allied landings in North Africa and Sicily. Named supreme commander of Allied forces, he directed the D-Day landings in northern France and the subsequent liberation of Paris and advance into Germany. His popularity was reflected by his election in 1952 as the 34th president of the United States, a position he held for 12 years.

Goebbels, Joseph

Nazi leader. Joseph Goebbels was the head of Nazi Party propaganda and later became minister of propaganda in the Nazi government. He used mass media and cinema skilfully to promote Nazi views. At the end of the war, he killed his children and committed suicide with his wife.

Hirohito

Emperor of Japan. Hirohito reluctantly approved the growth of army power and the militarization of Japanese society. He also backed the aggressive foreign policy that eventually led to war, but in 1945 he supported the leaders who wanted to surrender unconditionally. After the war he gave up his divine status and became a constitutional monarch.

Hitler, Adolf

Dictator of Germany. After serving as a soldier in World War I, Adolf Hitler joined a minor political party that he renamed the National Socialist Workers' Party (Nazis). Hitler was elected as chancellor of Germany in 1933 and became leader (Führer) in 1934. His policies were based on anti-Semitism and anti-communism, militarism, and the aggressive expansion of Germany. His invasion of Poland in September 1939 sparked the outbreak of the war. Hitler's war leadership was erratic and contributed to Germany's eventual defeat; Hitler himself committed suicide in his bunker in Berlin in the last days of the war.

Hope, Bob

U.S. entertainer. Comedian and singer Bob Hope was one of the biggest movie stars at the start of the war. He became famous for his constant tours of U.S. overseas bases to put on shows for service personnel. Having performed similar tours in later wars in Korea, Vietnam, and the Persian Gulf, Hope was acknowledged in 1997 by the U.S. Congress as the first "Honorary Veteran" in U.S. history.

MacArthur, Douglas

U.S. general. A veteran of World War I, MacArthur commanded the defense of the Philippines against Japan in 1941 before becoming supreme Allied commander in the Southwest Pacific. He commanded the U.S. attacks on New Guinea and the Philippines. After the end of the war, he became supreme Allied commander of Japan and oversaw the country's rapid postwar recovery.

Miller, Dorrie

Miller was an African-American seaman who served at Pearl Harbor in December 1941. Although at the time African Americans were only allowed to serve as orderlies, his courage during the Japanese attack earned him the Navy Cross and made him a national hero.

Montgomery, Bernard

British field marshal. Montgomery led the British Eighth Army in North Africa, where it defeated Rommel's Afrika Korps, and then shared joint command of the invasion of Sicily and Italy. He collaborated with U.S. general Eisenhower on planning the D-Day landings in France, where he commanded all land forces; Montgomery went on to command an army group in the advance towards Germany, where he eventually received the German surrender.

Mussolini, Benito

Italian dictator. Mussolini came to power in Italy in 1922 promoting fascism, a political philosophy based on a militaristic form of nationalism. He led attempts to re-create an Italian empire with overseas conquests. Mussolini became Hitler's ally in 1936 and entered the war on the Nazis' side. Italian campaigns went badly in the Balkans and North Africa, however. When the Allies invaded Italy in 1943 Mussolini was sacked by the king; he became president of a puppet German republic in northern Italy. He was executed by Italian partisan fighters at the end of the war.

Rommel, Erwin

German field marshal. Rommel was a tank commander who led the Afrika Korps in North Africa and later led the defense of northern France against the Allied invasion. When he was discovered to be part of a plot to assassinate Adolf Hitler, he was forced to commit suicide.

Roosevelt, Franklin D.

U.S. president. Democrat politician Franklin Delano Roosevelt enjoyed a privileged upbringing before entering politics and becoming governor of New York. He first came to power as president in 1932, when he was elected to apply his New Deal to solve the worst problems of the Great Depression. Reelected in 1936 and again in 1940 he fully supported the Allies, offering supplies to help fight the Germans. He was reelected in 1944, the only president to be elected for four terms, but died in office shortly before the end of the war against Japan.

Rosie the Riveter

A fictional American worker who first appeared in a popular song but whose image then appeared on posters and stamps to encourage women to take industrial jobs during the war. The various depictions of Rosie were based on a number of specific individual workers.

Stalin, Joseph

Soviet dictator. Stalin was a Bolshevik from Georgia who rose to prominence for his skill as an administrator. In 1922 he became general secretary of the Communist Party of the Soviet Union founded by Lenin. Stalin introduced programs to encourage agriculture and industry and in the 1930s got rid of many thousands of potential enemies in purges, having them jailed or executed. Having made a pact with Hitler in 1939, he was surprised when Hitler invaded the Soviet Union in 1941 but rallied the Red Army to eventual victory. At the end of the war, he imposed Soviet rule on eastern Europe.

Yamamoto, Isoroko

Japanese admiral. Yamamoto was a visionary naval planner who planned Japan's attack on the U.S. base at Pearl Harbor and its early Pacific campaigns. He was killed when the Americans shot down his aircraft in 1943, alerted by decoded Japanese radio communications.

Glossary

Allies One of the two groups of combatants in the war. The main Allies were Britain, the Soviet Union, the United States, British Empire troops, and free forces from occupied nations.

antibiotic A medicine that can halt the spread of infection.

anti-Semitism A hatred of Jews and Judaism.

armistice A temporary halt in fighting agreed to by both sides.

armor A term referring to armored vehicles, such as tanks.

artillery Large weapons such as big guns and howitzers.

Aryan In Nazi propaganda, relating to a mythical master race of Nordic peoples.

Axis One of the two groups of combatants in the war. The leading Axis powers were Germany, Italy, and Japan.

blitzkrieg A German word meaning "lightning war." It referred to the tactic of rapid land advance supported by great airpower.

Bolsheviks Members of the Communist Party that took power in Russia after the 1917 Revolution.

casualty Someone who is killed or wounded in conflict, or who is missing but probably dead.

collaborator Someone who works with members of enemy forces who are occupying his or her country.

communism A political philosophy based on state control of the economy and distribution of wealth, followed in the Soviet Union from 1917 and in China from 1948.

corps A military formation smaller than an army, made up of a number of divisions operating together under a general.

counteroffensive A set of attacks that defend against enemy attacks.

empire A number of countries governed by a single country.

embargo An order to temporarily stop something, especially trading.

espionage The use of spies or secret agents to obtain information about the plans of a foreign government.

evacuation The act of moving someone from danger to a safe position.

Fascism A political philosophy promoted by Mussolini in Italy based on dictatorial leadership, nationalism, and the importance of the state over the individual.

garrison A group of troops placed to defend a location.

Holocaust The systematic German campaign to exterminate millions of Jews and others.

hygiene Following practices, such as keeping clean, that support the maintenance of good health.

independence The state of self-government for a people or nation.

infantry Soldiers who are trained to fight on foot, or in vehicles.

kamikaze Japanese for "divine wind"; the name refers to Japan's suicide pilots.

landing craft Shallow-bottomed boats designed to carry troops and supplies from ships to the shore.

Marine A soldier who serves in close association with naval forces.

materiel A word that describes all the equipment and supplies used by military forces.

morale A sense of common purpose and positive spirits among a group of people or a whole population.

occupation The seizure and control of an area by military force.

offensive A planned military attack.

patriotism A love for and promotion of one's country.

propaganda Material such as images, broadcasts, or writings that aims to influence the ideas or behavior of a group of people.

rationing A system of limiting food and other supplies to ensure that everyone gets a similar amount.

reconnaissance A small-scale survey of enemy territory to gather information.

resources Natural materials that are the basis of economic wealth, such as oil, rubber, and agricultural produce.

strategy A detailed plan for achieving success.

strongpoint Any defensive position that has been strengthened to withstand an attack.

siege A military blockade of a place, such as a city, to force it to surrender.

taxes Fees on earnings or financial transactions used by governments to raise money from their citizens.

troops Groups of soldiers.

war bonds A form of investment used by governments in wartime to raise money from savers.

Further Reading

Books

Adams, Simon. *Occupation and Resistance* (Documenting World War II). Wayland, 2008.

Black, Hermann. *World War II, 1939–1945* (Wars Day-by-Day). Brown Bear Reference, 2008.

The Blitz. World War II Replica Memorabilia Pack. Resources for Teaching, 2010.

Burgan, Michael. *America in World War II* (Wars That Changed American History). World Almanac Library, 2006.

Cross, Vince. *Blitz: a Wartime Girl's Diary, 1940–1941* (My Story). Scholastic, 2008.

Deary, Terry, and Mike Phillips. *The Blitz* (Horrible Histories Handbooks). Scholastic 2009.

Dowswell, Paul. *Usborne Introduction to the Second World War.* Usborne Publishing Ltd., 2005.

Gardiner, Juliet. *The Children's War: The Second World War Through the Eyes of the Children of Britain.* Portrait, 2005.

Heppelwhite, Peter. *An Evacuee's Journey* (History Journeys). Wayland, 2004.

Hosch, William L. *World War II: People, Politics and Power* (America at War). Rosen Education Service, 2009.

MacDonald, Fiona. *World War II: Life on the Home Front: A Primary Source History* (In Their Own Words). Gareth Stevens Publishing, 2009.

McNeese, Tim. *World War II: 1939–1945* (Discovering U.S. History). Chelsea House Publishers, 2010.

O'Shei, Tim. *World War II Spies.* Edge Books, 2008.

Price, Sean. *Rosie the Riveter: Women in World War II.* Raintree, 2008.

Price, Sean. *The Art of War: The Posters of World War II* (American History Through Primary Sources). Raintree, 2008.

Ross, Stuart. *The Blitz* (At Home in World War II). Evans Brothers, 2007.

Ross, Stuart. *Evacuation* (At Home in World War II). Evans Brothers, 2007.

Ross, Stuart. *Rationing* (At Home in World War II). Evans Brothers, 2007.

Tonge, Neil. *The Rise of the Nazis* (Documentary World War II). Rosen, 2008.

Wagner, Melissa, and Dan Bryant. *The Big Book of World War II: Fascinating Facts about World War II Including Maps, Historic Photographs and Timelines.* Perseus Books, 2009.

World War II (10 volumes). Grolier Educational, 2006.

World War II (Eyewitness). Dorling Kindersley, 2007.

Websites

www.bbc.co.uk/history/worldwars/wwtwo/
Causes, events and people of the war.

http://www.bbc.co.uk/schools/primaryhistory/world_war2/
Interactive information on what it was like to be a child during the war.

http://www.spartacus.schoolnet.co.uk/2WW.htm
Spartacus Education site on the war.

http://www.nationalarchives.gov.uk/education/worldwar2/
U.S. National Archives primary sources on the war.

http://www.historylearningsite.co.uk/WORLD%20WAR%20TWO.htm
History Learning Site guide to the war.

http://www.telegraph.co.uk/news/newstopics/world-war-2/
Daily Telegraph archive of articles from wartime and from the 70th anniversary of its outbreak.

www.war-experience.org
The Second World War Experience Centre.

www.ibiblio.org/pha
A collection of primary World War II source materials.

www.worldwar-2.net
Complete World War II day-by-day timeline.

http://www.iwm.org.uk/searchlight/server.php?change=SearchlightGalleryView&changeNav=home
Imperial War Museum, London, guide to collections.

Index